tackle box

To Mary Glenny

with great delight –

tackle box

Patti White

August 12, 2003

2001 Anhinga Prize for Poetry
Selected by Diane Wakoski

Anhinga Press, 2002
Tallahassee, Florida

Cover design, book design and production – C.L. Knight
Author photo – Dan Fitzstephens
Typeset in Bitstream Goudy Sans Light and Medium

Library of Congress Cataloging-in-Publication Data
Tackle Box by Patti White – First Edition
ISBN 0938078-71-2
Library of Congress Card Number: 2002101530

*This publication is sponsored in part by a grant from the Florida Department
of State, Division of Cultural Affairs, and the Florida Arts Council.*

Anhinga Press Inc. is a nonprofit corporation dedicated wholly
to the publication and appreciation of fine poetry.

For personal orders, catalogs and information write to:
Anhinga Press
P.O. Box 10595
Tallahassee, FL 32302
Web site: www.anhinga.org
E-mail: info@anhinga.org

Published in the United States by Anhinga Press, Tallahassee, Florida.
First Edition, 2002

For my mother, my sisters, and my brother
Cathy White, Chris White, Connie Poleson, and Joe White

CONTENTS

ACKNOWLEDGMENTS

"Our Lady of Perpetual Help Business School," "The Cipher," and "The Line Factory" appeared in *Hopewell Review*. "Heartworm" and "Tackle Box" appeared in *Arts Indiana*. "TRINITY," "Demeter," "The Line Factory," and "Tackle Box" appeared in *Forklift, Ohio*. "She Wears Ophelia's Dress" appeared in *RedRiverReview*. "The Love Zombies" appeared in *Literal Latte*. "The Elegant-Armed Anemone," "The Rain Crow, "The Respiration of the Pines," "Alphabet," and "Flambeaux" appeared in *The MacGuffin*. "The Children's Crusade" appeared in *The Ledge*. "Medical Advice" appeared in *Mississippi Review*. "The Tin Man" appeared in *The Common Review*. "Clouds" appeared in *Nimrod* and "Road Kill" appeared in *THE HEARTLANDS TODAY*.

Some of the poems in this manuscript were published in *Nausea is the Square Root of Muncie*, a locally-circulated journal: "Architecture," April 1992; "Circe's Swine" and "The Man O' War Motel," October 1992; "The Love Zombies," January 1993; "The Mission of the Coming Days," Spring 1993; "The Children's Crusade," Fall 1993; and "Road Kill," 1994.

Some of the poems in this manuscript were published in two locally-circulated chapbooks: "Demeter," "The Tin Man," "The Man O' War Motel," "A Massing of Planets," "Heartworm," "Circe's Swine," "At the Johnson Creek Tavern," "Dumpsters," "The Love Zombies," and "Low Hanging Moon" in *The Love Zombies*, Ricepaper Press, 1993; and "Missing in Action," "Architecture," and "Snow Outside Cafe Seiyoken" in *Missing in Action*, Nausea Publishing, 1992.

Passages from *Beowulf* in "Heorot" are from a translation by E. Talbot Donaldson in *The Norton Anthology of English Literature*, Fifth Edition.

My thanks to Eric Appleby, Matt Hart, and Joe Trimmer.

tackle box

THE TIN MAN

I walked dreaming through the salt marsh:

sawgrass, soft crustacean smells,
tidal pools shining silver,
the sky a weatherless white.

The tin man waited on the sand,
the bay spread wide behind him,

muscles curved like oyster shells
a sheen like oil on water
tracing the line of his jaw.

I set the picnic basket down between us;
the hinges fell open, the heavy lid fell back
the glittering objects inside spilled out:

razorsharp bread,
electroplated eggs,
clanking fruit,

ores, elements, alloys
geological sustenance
food that lasts.

He spoke slowly, as if rusted, a warning:
the occasional tooth, chipped by a kiss,
an arm gone purple from too eager contact
with the angles of his body, the emery cloth,
diamond-bit drills, the constant maintenance,
these would be the price of his metallic love.

I like a man with hard edges, I replied;
I like a man sculpted, welded, riveted
by desire; I like a man who shines
a man lubricated and polished; I said:
I like a man with intrinsic value.

Then we lay down on the grainy sand;
I called him my tinman, my axeman,
I praised his booming chest, the echo
chamber of his heart:

       and woke on marshy sheets,
with sawgrass twisted like leather straps,
like thin metal bands, like flexible knives
cutting and binding the flesh of my hand.

ALPHABET

Algiers, Louisiana seemed exotic, a dark sexy bayou where
Burroughs nailed together orgone accumulators. Crossing
cottonfields worked by convicts, they high-balled west,
driving through the nights half drunk with stars, writing.
Even the dark hills of Pennsylvania were estranged by
falling rain, the slick and slippery shale of memory.
Ginsberg sent love letters to everybody, regardless,
Huncke, Corso, garbled messages of semen, stamps
inching off the envelope toward California, toward
Jack, and in every line he's screaming out: angel!
Kerouac! the trains in the night! Lovelorn, he mailed
letters; Burroughs answered with persistent insects,
mugwumps conspiring to invade his head like police
nostalgic for torture, like eager surgeons, or lepers
off-loading dead skin in packages wired to explode,
posted traces of kisses from opium dens, the
queers and junkies eating oranges in Tangiers.
Rising poets remember them, read them, take
solace in the beat journey across America, in
the boys sleeping by the side of the word
under the hobo sky, dreaming against the
vanity of form, riding the rails down the line.
What language do they speak, what sweet
X-ray skeleton grammar, what tongue, the
young poets three generations later, tasting the
zest of Burroughs' oranges, in Algiers, wasting.

DEMETER

HE STOLE MY BABY. I heard her coming down Ninth Avenue
on a quiet Sunday morning, no traffic, no rain, I heard
her sweeping up like a windstorm, drawing strength
from the vacant street, her cry shearing off corners,
making windows shiver, knocking the crust off bricks.
HE STOLE MY BABY. There was no one on the street but women,
two old ladies crossing 43rd heading for the thrift shop
which wouldn't be open for another three hours, a teenager
picking over the fruit at the Korean stand, cutting brown leaves
off lettuce, no babies anywhere in sight, no thieves running,
no men for at least ten blocks. HE STOLE MY BABY. She didn't
say anything else, not who did it, not why, or when it happened,
how he came for the child or what sex it was but probably
a girl this entirely female morning, she just called out
in a flat tone of cosmic rage, mobile, intense, determined,
passing through the city like a plague, going to bring it down,
collapse it, rot the fruit right in the stand, going to strike
terror, defoliate the parks, bring the snow down in huge drifts,
going to freeze the trains right in the tunnels, going to stop
him as he creeps through the stations, carrying the child
through the turnstiles, waiting for transportation, hidden
under the city, afraid to return to the surface, clutching
the stolen child as the earth dries and cracks around him,
dropping roots onto the rails, withered by her mother love.

HEARTWORM

Dogs are troubled by parasites:

hookworm, roundworm,
tapeworm, whipworm,
heartworm.

Every dog in America must be medicated in summer
when mosquitoes deposit eggs beneath the skin
and blood carries tiny worms to vulnerable hearts:

six months after exposure, adult heartworms
linger in pulmonary arteries, blocking the flow.
Once infected, arsenic is the only cure.

These internal parasites wear down their hosts:
the dogs grow listless and decline, their blood
sucked away, nutrients appropriated by invading
organisms, coats dull from lack of protein.
This is a slow and subtle death.

Poodles, labrador retrievers, weiner dogs,
beagles, alsatians, chows, redbone hounds
all the dogs need their hearts protected.

Ivermectin, diethylcarbamazine citrate
disrupts the life cycle of the heartworm,
but even preventive measures can prove fatal:

adverse reactions include dilated pupils,
depression,
and a staggering gait;

collies frequently collapse,
a breed too sensitive for drugs.

I was at the vet last week; I spent some time
reading Heartgard pamphlets; now I'm worried.

Parasites flourish in flat grassy areas; in Indiana
I know my heart is compromised. I am preoccupied.
My breath catches, my throat is constricted,
my blood does not circulate.

Something palpable, something red and warm,
is present where no life should be.

Heartworm drives insistently
toward reproduction and reinfection.
It motivates savage rhythms,
collects the blood
into standing pools
that ripple with heat,
pulsates long into the night,
straining against muscle,
swelling, expanding,
colonizing every vein.

Victims suffer
persistent coughing,
difficult breathing, and
finally
congestive heart failure.

I am certain this is my medical destiny.

I can already feel pressure in the ventricles,
strange movement in my most precious organ.

LOW HANGING MOON

I

I sleep heavily under the full moon;
white light weighs me down. Dreams
are thick then, choking sensibility,
and when I wake they refuse to shift.
They enter memory as events, rich
with substance; they leave traces
on my body like crumpled sheets.

One hot and sticky full moon night,
I landed in China, safely, though
the pilot had screamed with fear.
Everything was alien, angry, remote.
Furniture crowded rooms flooded after rain;
fungus cascaded over smooth cream walls.
I walked barefoot through the scorpion field
to bring him a green world carved from jade.

When I woke, my hands trembled with the weight
of the smooth stone globe; my feet were stung red
from the careless path I had chosen.

II

The moon has no face when the wind blows
and I sleep as though my life depended
upon dreams. Winter drifts in through
summer windows, filling the cabin with snow;
soft furs drape my body and I watch the cards:
he has the winning hand, a royal heart flush.

When I turn over, and the cat murmurs displeasure,
I find the family waiting in the kitchen; I feed
them creamed corn and steak; the malicious
parking lot moves cars from place to place, and
confused, I hear his sister calling to me

just before we board the Greyhound bus, heading
west like Kerouac, running high across the Rockies,
wide through dust and desert, and we ride, entwined,
standing in the center aisle, gazing out the window,
embracing all the way to California.

III

I dreamed the last dream away from home.

I traveled down south to sleep, no curtains,
New Orleans, getting warmer every night,
and I closed my eyes against the rising sun:

they were blood oranges, bloodstones,
Creole dubloons, alligator scales;
they were buttons cut from hex dolls.

We married in a brown-dog courtyard. With pigeons.
Chalk marks on the concrete. Photos on the table.
Grimy pink satin dress. Spanish moss and gumbo.

His hips moved like the blues, we drank bourbon
and chicory coffee, he was slick as an oyster.

He was the voodoo prince of love.

I died before him. Azalea bloomed
and he came mourning to my grave,
weeping like wisteria, bending
to gather the earth, my dry body;

he tied feathers in his hair

he filled my skull with his charms
he wore my bones around his neck

he kept my spirit captive.
It was a Cajun wedding
body and soul.

HANGING HEART LAKE

Saskatchewan. Saskatchewan.

The wind scoops and scrapes the land.
The wind smooths the fevered grass.

Saskatchewan wind sweeps shadow and stones.

No shadows in Saskatchewan.
No dreams in Saskatchewan.

Stay away from the shield rock:
the wide plains and pine forests
the bogs and grayling creeks
are treacherous, Canadian.

Saskatchewan remembers the glaciers.

Ice like velvet in Saskatchewan.
Ice blue water in Saskatchewan.

The trees in Canada are cruel trees.
The trees in Canada are cruel trees.

Hearts hang from the trees like pinecones
in the forests of Saskatchewan.

Old loves fly north in summer like geese
and roost in the trees of Saskatchewan.

Canada geese mate for life.

Saskatchewan. Saskatchewan.

THE CHILDREN'S CRUSADE

It was a hot summer in France.
It was a hot summer in 1212,
after a fervent winter and spring.

Divine letters fell into the hands of shepherds.
Insects swarmed, virgins fainted, infants chanted
the holy name, meteors streaked across the sky.

The innocents set forth. Mothers wept to see their sons
walk away from the farm. Fathers counted one less mouth.
Fathers kissed their daughters' lips; mothers pressed sons
to their mild and milky breasts. The innocents set forth.

One band of crusaders climbed over the Alps to Italy.
Strangers touched them, praised them, stroked their limbs
as if to scrape glory from delicate skin, tore hair
from their holy heads to weave into rings; blessed them.

When they reached the Mediterranean they stopped. Dispersed.
Went home again. This time the strangers robbed them, raped
and ridiculed them, led them astray into blind passes,
left them for dead, maimed, mauled, beaten, betrayed.

The second band marched straight down France to Marseilles.
Generous sea captains provided transport: seven ships
to Jerusalem, seven ships for the holy war, the children
went on board. Two ships went down in a sudden storm,
the remaining five sailed to Alexandria, to Islam,
where the children were sold into slavery.

Seventy years later, in June of 1284, another hot summer,
a man with a silver flute passed through the town of Hamelin.
He piped a lovely tune, a watery and lucid tune, a silver song

to the children, a special song for the children, and they
followed him out of the town and they all disappeared.

For many generations, the people of Hamelin counted time
from the year the children went missing. The big flood
came 17 years after the loss of the children. A plague hit
43 summers after the one when the children left. Crops failed

every tenth season for a hundred years
from the time the children were stolen away.

Late at night in Manhattan, I hear their pattering feet,
the tiny legions in their nightwear, underwear, slips
and pajamas, t-shirts and diapers, their rompers and
their princess dresses, following the piper, on crusade,

their innocence on display and in danger. Their small feet
beat a path in the asphalt to the bus terminal, its concrete
a welcome haven, an adult place, with tickets and restrooms.
They crowd on board and disappear into the American night.

I don't know how to count time now.

The children keep passing, lured away, enticed, tricked,
tempted, coerced, forced, held at gunpoint, bundled on board.

They keep looking at the country, marking the glass
with sticky fingers, forgetting their families,

they keep still under the spell of the silver flute,
they obey the kindly driver, they trust the adults,
they think the ship will take them to the one true cross.

SNOW OUTSIDE CAFE SEIYOKEN

Silence degree zero.
Not absence: incapacity.
Inoperable air.

AT THE JOHNSON CREEK TAVERN

Chip has just been made Chairman of the Board
of the Better Business Bureau
of a prosperous oceanside Southern town

and he's at the tavern with his folks
eating fried shrimp, fried okra, fried potatoes,
his golf-green sweater expanding, his jeans tight,
his thigh twitching under the table, his face red
and grinning, his hair cropped close to his scalp.

He tells them he's been a bad boy, having too much fun,
he tells them about the tailgate parties, cases of beer,
the jacuzzi at the beach house, the women, the girls,

the sweet young things,
and his momma says, Oh Chip.

Then he makes an announcement.
He says, I'm only twenty-five
and already chairman.

It's hard to get in, an involved process,
it takes an application, $400, references,
you must convince the board you're worthy
to be a leader of the business community.
He got in and they made him chairman. Yes,

Chip is hanging with the big boys, the big wigs,
he's making valuable contacts in chemicals, in banks,
in airport transportation. And he's only twenty-five.

He's moving into lumber soon, pinewood and turpentine.
His father knows the right man, he knows the name; he says,
Tell him you're my son and the doors will open for you.
His momma says, Just tell them who your daddy is.

Chip's daddy has been staring at me all night.
He thinks the lesbians have invaded the South
(I'm wearing a flannel shirt and no make-up);

he's thinking one good fuck would cure me
and I'm thinking
one good fuck would make this vacation complete.

But not with Chip. He sits so fine and arrogant.

No way that body could bend to a woman. Not even
a sweet young thing with Merle Norman lips, a tan,
and pale concealer glistening under her eyes.

But he's a fine prospect, that boy. Money,
confidence, Southern charm, a golden future
in a prosperous oceanside town on the move.

Now you can call Chip any time you want to.
He has an 800 number digital pocket-sized beeper.
Just tell him who your daddy is. He'll want to know.

CIRCE'S SWINE

There were 30 days of rain in July.

A summer enchanted or cursed
the corn rotting in the fields.

The 4-H exhibits were withdrawn
on the second day of the county fair;
farm boys huddled in the stock barns
damply lusting, smelling the heat of the cattle
and the dark musk of the sheep, staring across
the severing sheets of rain
at the goddess in the Masonic food stand.

The graveled parking lot, empty and strange,
seemed like a tenuous island in the sea,
uncertain of continuity, liable to disappear
in the mist beginning to rise from the earth;

the rides ran wet and dangerous, slick and
shining like the skin of sorcerers. The ring toss
offered sodden rabbits and goldfish flashing
lonely and silent in clear plastic bags.

Everything was swimming in rainwater.
The double Ferris wheel, the Gravitron,
the first-aid station, the Tempest.

And the swine were on the move. In the barns
the prize animals were to be auctioned off
and they came out to bathe under hoses;
the food vendors all had pork products:
ham and beans, chops, barbecued ribs,

giant tenderloins with mayonnaise on buns.
One pig carcass sprawled on the roaster

as if it were trying to climb out,
its hide crispy, snout charred,
eye sockets black with blood

as if one of the sailors had escaped,
run snorting and cavorting into the sea,

then thought better of facing the storm
and turned back to the enchanted isle

turned and struggled and kicked and paddled
and heaved his heavy body onto the shore at last

only to be struck by lightning.

LITERAL DREAMS

Zig-zagging lightning-struck pines.
Yellow pollen falls in clouds, and
X-ray skeleton shadows stripe the
wet fields of granite and sage.
Viral stars hover, rotor-blades
unwinding the night, the air
tap tap taps as it meets the street, and
sleet melts into the gutter in rippled
rat-tails of water and litter.

Queasy hamburger and fries, a Coke,
please hurry with the food; there's an
orange marmalade cat in the window,
neatly observing. Don't move, don't
move — the police are at the door,
looking for Jimmy Hoffa, for
Kennedy, for murderers not yet named.

Jade plants twist in the wind, dropping
inky suggestions to succulent neighbors and
here beyond the creek the weasels dig,
generous to a fault, laboring with faux
fur matted, the dens filling with bones, until
every river bend is blocked with chalk, and

driven to madness, the cleaning women
call out, abusing the pillows, dusting
behind the bed-frame, re-setting the
alarm to Eastern Standard Time.

FOR THOSE WHOSE BODIES ARE NEVER FOUND

I tracked that cat like a lover gone missing.
I walked the streets with mist coming down,
with light dropping from windows

as heavily as stones. When the mist froze
I skated, cracking surface ice, leaving
pressure in patterns behind me.

I stalked Ira through the neighborhood,
invaded privacy, peering into living rooms,
hiding in bushes; I crossed the creek,

I looked, I called, I cruised,

I boxed that subdivision, quartered it
east and west, north and south; I drove

late into the night, braking for every shadow,
flipping on the high beams, going slow.

***

Keeping very still

breathing as the snow breathes
as frozen earth breathes

freezing into place

imprinting visual information
expanding the range of my ears
the blood sinking in my organs

sitting silent as a crystal

keeping faith with the mystery,
believing in the restitution of love,

knowing that it won't be simple,
knowing that ice breaks hard, that

when cats come out of the blizzard
they will move as ghosts, with snow
draped over their shoulders, gracefully
furred like Russians, self-conscious

and delicate about their feet. That is
how cats travel in the snow. Hesitantly.
Softly. Obsessively. Refusing many things.

* * *

He crouched by an enormous tree,
catching his breath, steaming, leaning
against the trunk thick and dark as lava,
the branches overhead plunging, the leaves
flashing, blanching, stripping free,
a tree as tall as Yggdrasil, the rune tree,
the tree of Fate, the tree that roots the world.

He stood streaming sweat, wet from the rain,
soaked black by water, swept naked by the wind;
his eyes were shining with storm
strange with vision, wild with running
and his cat smile curved up sharply

as I caressed his body,
stroking hot muscles, tracing the pulse points,
touching the diagonal of his jaw with my lips
biting gently on the bone there, licking the rain.

Then the wind took the tree,
lightning scratched the sky with broken claws
and the storm shrieked like panthers, cats screaming
around us in the darkness with the tree down
and the earth unrooted and spinning loose.

✳✳✳

I drive the highway on an impassive fall day,
the sky etched in pewter and chalk, the road dry,
the shrubs and weeds gone mustard, gone claret,

tracking, hunting, creating a routine,
mapping images on windshield cave walls,
writing with sticks and bones, with blood,

sketching with charcoal and clay, tracing power,
marking out the one animal, the prized animal,
the animal sacred to the clan, totem, the loved one

carving the concrete like a Viking glyph,
spying Odin's runes from the world tree
elk horns for defense, the ox for strength

driving in a religious frenzy, devoted to the road,
wearing it down like a holy stone kissed by pilgrims

carrying an icon on the dashboard, a small fetish
of fur and hide twisted, making the way clear

driving the highway beyond the limits of sorcery,
of ritual, beyond desire, beyond grief, too far.

✳✳✳

Some things just disappear. Mist closes in and they're gone.
November comes, and the year has slipped away. Nights pass
and half your life is over before you know it.

I still drive through the neighborhood I think of as Ira's,
pretending he has found a home with some indulgent family,
that he grows fat on table scraps; or that he joined the gang
of wild cats living in the junkyard; that he went on the road,
a silky cat Kerouac, drinking out of ditches, gone to Colorado
searching for his father, his fluffed-out relatives in the hills.

Of course he must be dead; frozen at thirty-below
on the first night of the blizzard; run over by a car;
the outside world is hard on cats, those soft creatures.

I searched everywhere but never found the body.

Tomorrow will be the first snow of the new winter;
today I drew the blank rune, sign of the unknowable,
and released the old one at last, the journey rune,
Raitho the rune of obsession, the rune of riding

the rune for the passage of dead souls,
the journey charm, the rune for riding.

THE LOVE ZOMBIES

We scorched them the night they came through.
We burned the cornfields under their feet,
poured gasoline down the rows and tossed matches.
They just kept on, lurching toward the farmhouse;
the sheriff said it was love that drew them,
he said they were greedy for the taste of love.

Their need was insatiable, terrible. Dire.
I saw one stop, stop and spread his arms wide
embracing the corn, hugging it to his breast,
so hungry for love he would hold dry stalks
like a cherished woman, so lonely he would
walk through fire to approach a living heart.

The sheriff followed them down the road, blue lights
flashing on their charred coats, siren wailing softly;
we stepped back to let them pass. Blackened, ashy,

they walked barefoot on gravel, on hot coals,
dragging gunny sacks of mementos behind them:

livers, knuckle bones, pressed flowers,
tin can lids, movie tickets, gallstones,
umbrella ribs; moving slow as threshers,

they shuffled along the fenceline, stumbling blind,
away from our precious farms. We never knew
where they went after we burned them out.

I guess they blended with the population;
I guess they went underground in the cities
traveling through utility tunnels, tracing
steam pipes to exclusive apartments, watching
church weddings and old musicals, hiding

behind newspapers, waiting on park benches,
feeding on pizza crusts, feeding on memories,

dreaming of the tiny shoots of green corn,
the lettuce, the spinach, romaine, cool thin leaves
between their toes, dreaming of fullness, the grain
of love swelling their stomachs, hunger satisfied,
life replenished, the cornfields waving to them
across the smoky past, the farmers with open arms,
the harvest ready to be gathered, the hunger
satisfied, the love sheriff leading them home.

THE MAN O' WAR MOTEL

People bring the consequences of their obsessions
to the Man O' War Motel: they commit suicide here
and murder their favorite daughters; they sit on the bed
drinking vodka; they flush blood down the toilet;
they stare at cheap prints of Paris and think about cancer;

they call old lovers and threaten to kidnap their dogs,
or to visit next Christmas with heroin and syphilis;

they plot assassinations and write pornography;
they work jigsaw puzzles and wait for the FBI.

The Man O' War Motel was built after the big war:
an office and fourteen rooms just off the highway,
Kentucky limestone, modern conveniences, red neon.
Nobody knows your business here but yourself.

This is where you go when you're on the lam,
on welfare, on drugs you can't afford,
when your husband walks out or goes to jail,
when the IRS wants to talk very seriously
about last year's income, and the CIA inquires
about the terrorist you met in Italy this summer.

The Man O' War Motel has chickens in the yard,
a rusty blue T-Bird up on blocks, potholes
in the parking lot, curtains gone gauzy with age.
The Man O' War has seen better days. In fact

Lolita slept here. She ran across America
day after day in the car with Humbert, sticky
with bribery sweets, fuzzy with puberty,
blurred from being licked and kissed
and handled, tired out with revulsion.

And when they got to the Man O' War she fell into bed
and slept deeply, the blankets scratching her face,
the motion of the road still rocking her body.
In the morning she woke and knew she was home,
among the lost and the vagrant, the desperately transient;

she knew that no matter how soiled her youth had become
here were souls who had fallen farther, lives more sordid
and infinitely less literary, and she felt clean and free
for just that one morning, though she had another hundred
motels, tourist cabins, and motor courts to sleep in
before the end of the novel, and Humbert still had the keys
and they were jangling over her head after breakfast.

ARCHITECTURE

So I'm walking down Eighteenth Street
and I see this perfectly formed mouse
flattened on the pavement.

Its legs are radiant, a weathervane
marking the cardinal compass points.

And it's dry and smooth, no guts exposed;
the skeleton is crushed under the fur.
It's thinned to an oval disc.
A skipping stone. A subway token.

Which reminds me of the night
I walked down Ninth Avenue
after the opera, eleven o'clock,
and I pass this girl crying
pressed into a doorway and
her whole body fits into that space
the three inches depth of the frame.

And I see that things get squeezed
in the gravity well of the city

that solid things implode from stress
and the density of air in confinement
bears down on every structure

and I think of Archimedes in his bathtub
and the displacement of water by mass

and I imagine the Chrysler Building
stepping into the tub, its silver rays
half-mooned above the gargoyles

and I think of the weight of the city
heavy on its granite foundation
and that even rock compresses over time

and I see the water level rising
as buildings sink into the glassy bay

and the gargoyles gazing up through the water
as the girl floats free down the alley

and when the rivers east and west
cross, collide, and close

I see the furry disc of the flattened mouse
drifting like a leaf upon the waves.

OUR LADY OF PERPETUAL HELP
BUSINESS SCHOOL

has premises under the 59th Street Bridge,
looks abandoned, derelict, bereft; holds
night classes funded by faith; guarantees
miraculous advancement. It calls to mind
a placard on the E-train that says:

THE VIRGIN MARY HAS A MESSAGE FOR QUEENS.

Sister Catherine Ignatius Loyola Fortunata
teaches computer science; amber screens
cast halos behind her as she glides, bends,
touches a key, interprets a command. She knows
the language: she can access the mystery.

Sister Catherine Ignatius Loyola Fortunata
thinks the Virgin Mary is in the computer
at Our Lady of Perpetual Help Business School.

She hears the hum of the motor
as the Holy Mother's lullaby;
accepts the pulsing prompt
as a manifestation of grace,
a divine intention to listen,
to intercede, to respond in kind.

Sister Catherine worships with authority:
she's gone beyond the binary universe,
good and evil, off and on, one and zero.
She writes software; she understands
the third position, the ghost in the machine.

Sister Catherine guides her students in ritual,
in routines that protect them from fatal mistakes:

they memorize passwords,
they never erase the hard drive,
they do not bring drinks to the lab.

Sister Catherine's students file documents
in subdirectories.

The modem gives the Virgin Mary
access to the Bell System: on the 25th
of every month, Mary leaves a message
on the Mira-call answering machine.
She has an 800 number.

CNN recently reported that since 1830
only seven apparitions of the Virgin Mary
have been authenticated by the church;
none of these have been in the United States.

But the Mira-call line claims that Queens
was graced by the Virgin eleven years ago,
and that must be when she set things up:

the optical fibers of New York Bell,
the modem at Perpetual Help,
an answering machine and a mailing address
in Arkansas.

Mary records her message of peace
and conducts real-time conferences
at the business school, interfacing,
hearing the prayers of young women.

She was herself a bookish woman,
who was impregnated by words.

The angel Gabriel spoke
and she was with child.

Sister Catherine Ignatius Loyola Fortunata
asks the Virgin Mary to process information;

Sister Catherine adores Mary's

channel capacity, her facility for translation,
her ability to enact complex transformations.

But sometimes
sometimes an encounter with the computer
produces an electricity, an ecstasy in her bones:

the monitor flashes white, scrolls the text,
displays the gospel on a field of virgin blue;
programs engage, emerge, and Catherine thrills
to the vibration of pure communication.

          Privately (she does not confess it)
Sister Catherine Ignatius Loyola Fortunata considers
this an immediate experience of glory, direct revelation,
epiphany, the gift of tongues, the key to all the codes.

CLOUDS

move like the earnest thoughts of right whales
ponderously through oceanic massy brains,
ideas about plankton, notions of sperm,
the high caloric fat of mammary dreams,
stark amazement at the silvery flash of sardines
too many to count, too quick to define
the yawning mouth containing their substance.

The whales, white and gray, think philosophy,
argue autonomy, debate cosmology, cogitate
on the possibility of life on earth. Could the dry
land support such deep and heavy thinkers;
could they orate across air as easily as in liquid?

Sometimes they question universal ontology
suspecting that no purpose sustains them,
that their passage leaves no trace in the sea,
that all whales are simply unceasing thought,
a soft drifting of clouds over the surface of the sky
with nothing beneath them that will remain.

TACKLE BOX

People who fish have a peculiar love for equipment,
for paraphernalia, for spatial coordinates,
trajectories, for the tension between surface and depth.

People who fish know there is more to water
than can be seen by the naked eye, more to a lure
than shape and dazzle, more to filleting than a long
sharp knife; people who fish are patient, dedicated;
they understand the relation between desire and deed.

Down in South Florida, an old couple fished together
for fifty years in the green water of the salt bays,
the black water of springs in turpentine country,
the wide flat saucer of Okeechobee, the sweet rivers,
the brackish mangrove swamps, the shallow Gulf where
big rays come to breed in August, the Everglades,

fifty years on the waters of Florida, fifty years
of setting traps for bait, filling the thermos with
morning coffee, checking the barometer, scaling fish.

She had precise notions about ordering her tackle;
she kept her hooks sharp, her bloodstained stringer
neatly wound and stored; she had her own supplies:
Bandaids, Maalox, Teaberry gum, leaders, sinkers,
ten pound test line, red and white bobbers, Coppertone,
aspirin, antibiotic cream, nitroglycerin pills,

so it made sense to him, when she passed away,
to keep her ashes in her tackle box, for love.

One afternoon two thieves came to the trailer
when the old man was away and couldn't believe their luck.

They came for electrical appliances, carelessly displayed
credit cards or checks, maybe a gold watch or a wedding ring
left lying on the sink after washing up; petty thieves, young,
they came for the obvious, the quick sell to the fence

and found a metal box full of drugs near a rusty bait bucket.

They bolted from the trailer and went directly to Castroville
where Jesus Huerfano purchased the drugs for a reasonable
but not extravagant sum; the thieves walked away with cool cash
and two small packets of white powder for a treat later on.

Jesus made it a rule to sample his product and when he sniffed
he felt the rush, a rather strange sensation, rather glittery,
but certainly, clearly, a chemically induced alteration,
so the drugs went on the street that evening.

Oh that bone cocaine, the soft ash,
so fine, so white, so

insidious. Two weeks later a stock broker found himself
drawn to the Wal-Mart where he stood staring at the lures
for half an hour, the plastic crabs, fluorescent shrimp,

the Bass Rat, Orange Poppers, the Super Guido Frog,
the Rebels, Rappalas, the Mepps Black Fury,
the Daredevils, Silver Minnows, Scattering Shad,

the 6" Twirl Tail Worms. The merchants in town were surprised
by a run on waders, surf rods, and insect repellent. Charters
rented out to oddly inept men, sniffling trollers whose
needle-marked arms burned in the sun, teenagers
driving BMWs lurked near marinas, and two bait shops

were looted on Sunday night. The two thieves
signed up on a drift boat and worked the season.

And Jesus Huerfano had dreams of glistening fish

skipjacks and mullet, sheepshead, silvery sea trout,
mysterious redfish, grouper, flounder, and tarpon

he dreamed of fish head soup and grainy oysters
of deep fried snapper throats and conch fritters

he dreamed of soft white sand at the bottom of the sea
and glittering bones that shifted, drifted, so gently,
with the pull of the waves overhead

he dreamed of shining bones
dancing in the current as the fish sailed by.

TALL YELLOW GRASS

takes the wind by giving
in total submission,
whispers: *I will cut you*
as the air glides and presses
on its thin dry body.

A suicide blonde bound to the earth,
just a generation past the prairie,
it takes the wind like a beating,
it never seeks shelter, never cracks,
never calls the police, always asks for more.

Grass bends to the force of insistent air
and remains standing, still thin,
shivering in high heels and lipstick
piercing the tongue of the wind
with sharp and narrow desire.

MEDICAL ADVICE

She said:
darlin', you know what it's like to be a woman.
The moon is always draggin' your body around,
and it seems like something is always wrong.

I was in here last year, and the doctor said:
that's weird: your cervix is awfully close

and I thought about that all year long
and thought it must be some kind of cancer symptom
or else my uterus was fallin' out or near to that

so this year, when the doctor said: oh that's weird
I said: what do you mean, what do you mean, weird
what's wrong with my cervix? and the doctor said to me,

said, I swear to God, the doctor said: well,
well, it's not really the cervix at all, it's just

it's that your vagina is
well, it's
short.

Well. And what am I supposed to do with that information?
Get an extension?

I got to admit, it bothers me. Just how short is short?
I keep wanting to ask other women,

                    and sometimes at night
I think about calling up old lovers, you know
calling up and saying: do you remember inside
a sort of brick wall effect in the back?

Darlin', this is a major problem for me.
I lie awake thinking about having a baby
and I think: what if my vagina is too short?
maybe the baby needs to be squeezed into shape
as it travels down the birth canal, and my baby
wouldn't be traveling at all, it would just pop out
like out of that big chrome toaster my momma had.

well

there's a shortage of sperm donors in my part of town anyhow
you know the men have all gone gay; there's no manly men left;
nobody wanting to be a father or love a woman

and I expect those old boyfriends think they're really hung
hitting the back wall like that every time

but I got to say I'm just tired of folks tellin' me
about my body, tired of the moon, tired of blood
and water and pains that nobody can name; darlin'

you know what it's like to be a woman?
and I said: yes I do. I know.

THE CIPHER

*"Hello. You've reached the Miller residence — but no one lives
here anymore." A telephone message recorded by Ann M. Miller
before she killed herself, her two children, three dogs, and
parakeet last week.*   — Newsweek, *September 27, 1993*

She learned her numbers late in childhood.

The apples and oranges were tangible,
useful, obvious: add one, have more;
subtract one and one classmate goes hungry;
take them all away, have nothing left.

But the numerals carried no weight.
Six plums minus one left five plums

but 6 - 5 equaled another numeral
and no fruit at all.

Story problems tortured her at night.
She figured the meeting of two trains
and one very fast bird as a tragedy
instead of three separate equations;

she wanted to know *when* the slow freighter
came to be filled with cameras and

why Farmer Jones sowed wheat and corn
in a rectangular field formerly planted
with pumpkins, sunflowers, and beans.

Algebra was worse than acne. That X cubed plus Y cubed
should be the same as XY cubed was incomprehensible;
anyone could see that X and Y were different, and n,
as a representative of the very concept of number
forced her from the room in tears.

Square roots made her shiver: the radical
scraped like a knife along her nerves;

she hated fractions, arcs, sine and cosine,
axioms, theorems, transfinite numbers,

she loathed the Barber paradox, the Cantor paradox,
Godel's numbers, Fermat's Last Theorem,
trap-door functions, singularities,
and the Rashomon effect. Babylonian notation,

the spread of the zero from India like a plague,
the algorithmic calculation named for Al-Khowarizmi,
the ritual geometry of the Beaker People,

all these were as nothing to her
and she cheated on every test she took.

The evidence suggests, however, that one concept
made a powerful impression, that she remembered

set theory, which depends upon pattern recognition,
the impermeability of logical borders, that apples
and only apples belong in the enamelware bowl,

that things which share characteristics
share a common intellectual location

and a common fate, that possession is eternal,
that relation is unbreakable so long as the brackets hold

a theory prizing consistency, membership, and collection
even under conditions of the most stringent subtraction

so that when the apples have all been eaten,
the set of the cores has a family likeness

and no boundary has been violated
no trespass has occured.

A WATERCOLOR BY HENRY BITTLE

The countryside is volcanic
a watery blue horizon struck dumb
by peaks picked out in green.
A little farm crouches close
to a half-eaten jungle, a sinister sun
beats down on mules and wild dogs,
bleaches the thatch on out-buildings,
soaks the animals in sweat. Inside
the house just right of the frame
a man is reading Dickens, his fingers
tracing each line, his mouth forming
words, his breath a humid gloss on humid shade.

In the novel, Betsy Trotwood wages war on donkeys
and this single link draws the man in
to a world without lava, without palm trees,
a climate for roses, a market for sugar.
The donkeys in Dickens do not work in the fields,
but the man knows them, their sturdy backs,
their reluctance, their diseases, the way they want
to lie down in the afternoon sun, how they pull against
the load, how they smell in the evening when the man
whispers to them, his lips close to their soft ears,
how the ear turns to catch each syllable, tracing his
words as he traces the lines in Dickens, the donkeys
and Dickens meeting there on the edge of the jungle,
with a volcano promising revolution, and the rising moon
tracing the blades of the palms, the edge of the house,
all the lines like a watercolor painted by an American
who knows nothing at all about donkeys, nothing about Dickens.

RADIATION

Radiation compels a clarity,
an essential penetration: vital
particles exert pressure, extend
to invade alien elements, pierce
natural objects, enter otherness.
Inside the reactor, events begin
to accelerate: proximate atoms
shift positions, collide; coincidence
generates density — two plain stones,
radically unlike, find mutual release
in ultimate decomposition —
fission — decay, the final collapse
of cohesion, of internal order —
the admission of chaos as bliss.

WARBLE

for Charles Bukowski

A cross bleak kiss
scabs her lower elbow.
He unlaces silk curses;
each veil has larks below.

She scares horses.
So rash, his crush,
a slow brick scowl.

MISSING IN ACTION

*We dropped millions of leaflets over Vietnam, Laos, and Cambodia
promising to pay $5,000 in gold to anyone who could provide us
with information leading to the recovery of a missing American in
Southeast Asia.*

> — *Lt. Col. Horace J. Reisner*
> *USAF, Retired*
> *Atlantic, April 1992*

I plan to claim that reward
for I have found the lost soldiers

and now I realize the homeless vets
working the concrete rice paddies
and patrolling Broadway at night
are diversionary forces sent forward
to conceal the action behind the lines.

Here are the coordinates:

40 degrees 12 minutes North
85 degrees 23 minutes West.

I plan to inform the authorities.

One night, on reconnaissance myself,
I discovered the garrison of the lost.

A quiet neighborhood in the heartland.
A middling sort of place without distinction.

When I approached the perimeter
guided by a string of bare bulbs
that reached from pole to porch

I saw their pickup truck
painted for camouflage
license plate: POW

their dark camper
labeled: NAPALM

and a female torso in fatigues
propped against cans of gas
and rainwater: legless, plastic.
Hands shiny pink. Saluting.

The house was a fortress.
Stockade fence around the deck;
trenches across the front yard.

The windows were taped and papered;
no light passed in any direction.

I have to wonder what they do in there:
read *Soldier of Fortune*, study maps,
plot campaigns against the East Side,

enumerate the missing.

I remember a house taped and papered
in Colorado; three men and their woman
heavy into drugs, selling plasma for cash

murdered a friend one summer. They held
him captive in the house for a week
beat him senseless, starved him

then took him up Gold Camp Road
in the middle of the night

stabbed him 67 times
and he refused to die

the bayonet kept striking bone

67 times and he finally bled to death
and was left draped around a jackpine
on the south slope of the mountain.

When detectives entered the
taped and papered house
the walls were covered with blood,
vomit, urine, Clorox, and beer.

The windows were sealed.
No light escaped in any direction.

So I wonder what goes on behind the paper
in this quiet neighborhood in middle America.

I plan to claim my reward.
I have found the missing veterans
who never came back from the war.

They are gathered in the drop zone
three houses up from a living room
with papier-mâché rabbits in the window

two blocks away from a backyard
piled five-feet high in
lumber, appliances, and egg cartons

across the creek from a power station
generating lethal magnetic forces;
they are staging random operations

drilling their troops
discussing strategy
mining the driveway.

Their landlord is getting worried.
He is afraid of explosions,
of finding dead cats stacked
like cordwood in the garage;

he won't know what to tell the police.

When the lost soldiers pull out
his house will be bleached — or bloody

there will be craters in the yard
the string of lights will be shot out
with the last of the ammunition

and the house will be littered with messages
asking for supplies for uniforms and boots
for food for weapons for nuclear missiles

the house will be papered with messages
from the shock troops camped in New York.

SHE WEARS OPHELIA'S DRESS

She wears Ophelia's dress
wrung out and hung to dry
on the frame of her shoulders.
Or what, perhaps, the creek saw
as it gazed up at a surface
broken, shattered by flesh,
the watery trees and golden herbs
floating around her like cloth
woven so fine as to be transparent.
Had Ophelia lived, she would someday
have owned a dress that, like this one,
appeared as a poetry of thread, a thin tapestry,
a field beneath a face, rosemary for remembrance.

THE ELEGANT-ARMED ANEMONE

They were natives of the tidal pool, the anemones,
anchored to rock, great colonies in the shallows,

fantastically shaped, marvelously tinted,

rose pink, topaz, violet flesh
frilled, folded, flounced

swelling stalks of flesh,
rippling tongues of flesh,
transparent fingers of flesh,

acid green and yellow curves
fringed tunnels, plush mouths

billowing, swaying, dancing flesh
pressed and washed by the restless sea

until some spirit moved them
and they began to migrate

inland.

Many anemones settled in Canada,
in Vancouver, for the roses,
the fog, and the voluptuous name.

The hardier species pushed deep into the prairie
and bent their soft spines to the plow, raising
cattails and reeds, swamp cabbage and watercress.
Others invaded the forest, surrounding the pines
with antithesis.

Now, in the night, the north wind
soughs like a tide through milk white tentacles
and anemone spores sweep southward on the current,
identical, miniature, moonfaced, delicate. Oh

think how the land has been enhanced by the sea:
high in the mountains, the elegant-armed anemone
offers its translucent embrace, it beckons, it curls

and the gray wolves leave the shelter of the trees
as if swimming into thin sweet air, seeking the touch,
the caress of a creature that never had a bone
or a solid thought,

the pines dream of the fluttering leaves they were denied,
the boulders shift, contracting and expanding toward flesh,
and the hard ground shudders, it roars with delight.

THE LINE FACTORY

Blue collar work. Metal lunch buckets. Low pay.
The women all dyed their hair blonde in 1965.
The men lived best and hardest in the army.

The factory was built of Indiana limestone;
it draws water from artesian wells, sends out
a permanent tornado of steam, gathers up
full silos of shavings, ships carloads of product.

Laborers in three shifts keep the lines moving:
straight lines, triangles, french curves, plumb lines,
lines parallel and skewed, trap lines, rulers.

This is where grocery lines are formed,
where picket lines are stored; here are

old latitudes recycled, pure borders distilled, time zones
fitted and polished, squall lines stacked for transport,
fine lines drawn, broad strokes forged, monoclines tilted;

striations, stripes, strings, and streaks
sedimentary layers, variegations, margins

columns, files, edges, bands, dashes, strips
tracing paper, sequences, alignments

designed, manufactured, and warehoused,
invented, fabricated, and repaired.

This is where sidewalk cracks are scored into cement,
where bloodlines are connected, section lines surveyed;

this is where lifelines are etched into skin,
where the equator was hammered out
like a great copper bracelet round the earth.

That was a miracle of engineering, the equator,
a line so grand in concept that workers wept
when the prototype was extruded, so massive
in production that ordinary cranes and tools
were useless, so compelling in construction
that contractors finished projects early,
foremen refused raises, and inspectors
waived all safety regulations in perpetuity.

Former steelmen handled the high grade lineage
as it melted in enormous vats; sophisticated rollers
thinned the magma into uniform sheets ready to cool;
ceramic ball bearings carried the plates to be cut,
to be tooled, to be shaped and soldered into a vast ring,
a circle, an absolute division of north and south, a line.

Each segment was measured by laser, by computer,
by handmade arcs carved from heartwood;
each segment was stress-tested, laminated;
every inch was oiled and wrapped in cotton wool
pending completion of the whole.

After delivery, and installation, and a surreptitious nighttime test,
a ribbon-cutting ensued, attended by foreign dignitaries,
who already objected to certain rate schedules,
by government lapdogs, who found the occasion redundant,
and by one factory representative, who seemed reluctant
to discuss the physics behind the success of the project.

On that day, back in Indiana,

restoration work was beginning on a series of fault lines;
countless mundane orders were quietly filled;
laborers ate lunch from metal lunch buckets
as the equator tightened to the girth of the globe:
25,000 miles, perfect, wholesale, factory direct.

FLOATING ISLAND

A custard of mangrove, matted, rootless.
Alligators like raisins drift toward clumps
of clotted eggs and egrets, nutmeg snakes.
No weather troubles the passing of the day.

ROAD KILL

*Her decomposed body was found Thursday buried under some
leaves in a wooded area near the rest area parking lot.*
> — Muncie Evening Press, *June 13, 1992*

Someone is killing the prostitutes
on Interstate 70. Leaving them

strangled in drainage ditches
suffocated on entrance ramps,
naked in rest areas that say:

no services.

The dead women worked the truck stops:
exit 201 E-Z off and on. Took MasterCard
and Visa. Made good money on the road. Then

some good old boy with calluses on his butt
and a rich red dick all raw from being rubbed
and a brain gone soft and foamy like warm beer
got a little rough one night. Squeezed tight
and watched her eyes bulge out. Said later

that he fucked one blind.
Did it again on the next run.

Now the hookers are scared. The draining boredom
of endless men in T-shirts and caps unzipping,
the rocking rhythm of sex on the road, the names
coming over the CB, modulations in sweat, in the
flavor of semen, in the size of the belly,
pretending to admire the truck, checking for sores,

lord these little routines seem sweet now,
compared to a killer working your territory.

He's got competition. Someone else
is killing the store clerks on I-70,

pale cashiers with deep purple lipstick,
part-timers at convenience stores. Girls
who get hypnotized by the ring of the register.

They call this execution style murder. A nervous
customer carries a gun in a paper bag, or tucked back
in his belt under his shirt; he orders something
that takes a little time, maybe a chocolate shake
and a burger with no pickles; the gun comes out
and he says: kneel down here, and: if you're quiet
you don't get hurt. Then he pulls the trigger.

You almost need warning signs: killer crossing.
Two men stalk the busiest east-west route in the country,
a third moves slowly north and south, leaving
red-haired women dead behind him, the latest a nun

formerly associated with the Sisters of Saint Benedict,
formerly a resident of Jeffersonville, Indiana,
formerly alive, expected to return to work, breathing.

The Interstate Homicide Squad keeps busy.
They push pins into maps and connect them with string.
They look for repeated patterns.

They publish photos of the dead prostitutes:
four mottled faces, two charcoal reconstructions
that say: REWARD FOR INFORMATION.

I think about the folks who have
stories to tell: the manager at McDonalds
the next car gliding into the Shell station
the trucker who found one under the bushes
the road crew cutting grass hitting flesh.

But mainly I think of killers and victims
traveling intersecting vectors of death;

I hear the doppler shift in the truck horns
passing the scene of the crime at high speed;

I see women frozen in the headlights
like rabbits fixed by their fear;

I feel the impact of the bullet
like a car smashing the brain.

They found the red-haired woman on Thursday.
Covered with leaves like a woodland creature.

Had she not been discovered
she would have returned to earth
following the logic of decay.

I've seen bodies on the road.

The small animals melt down
pounded and pressed thin
reduced to oil and fiber.

But the deer
the deer collapse

as if enchanted,
necks stretched,
limbs straight,

and they seem like women to me
falling into the deepest sleep
dreaming among the wildflowers.

THE MISSION OF THE COMING DAYS

Jesus would come to Asia first:
he would take us

out of small automobiles stalled in traffic;
he would lift old uncles off bicycles
dropped with wheels still spinning;

he would pull aunties up to heaven,
their string bags spilled open;

he would send street vendors aloft,
their grimy awnings flapping,
their kimchee steeping in the pot;

parasols would fly away end over end
and we would be gone to glory
leaving Seoul empty but for sinners.

The stock market would crash.
Factories would shut down.

Escalators would ascend with nobody aboard.
The city would halt in astonishment.

Jesus would enter Korea; so our pastor said.
We would be plucked up out of our lives

assumed bodily into paradise,
our prayers still on our lips,
words left hanging in the air;

the sinners would see our feet
dangling over their heads,

see our brows crowned with stars
as clouds concealed the opening gate
from the unworthy eyes still on earth.

Oh we believed.
We sold our cars.
We canceled leases.
We quit our jobs.

And Jesus did not come.

My old mother has a pair of oxen
yoked together to plow the fields;

when my father died she led them out
and turned the green rice under;

soil curved over the blade like water
and the crop bowed down to her grief.

I still believe in the rapture.
We are living in the last days
and the faithful will be taken up.

DUMPSTERS

I met her in the Public Library, reading Sir Thomas Wyatt,
the Elder, the Renaissance court poet you know, you know the one
about the deer, they flee from me, like how tourists scurry away
only in the poem it's the beggars, the lovers, the deer
who run after having fed, the deer refuse to return to his hand,
it's a sad story.

An educated woman, and a clean one: she bathes in the restroom
on the third floor; when she begs on 42nd Street she's a queen,
a rock in the current, impeccable, correct, her open palm
smooth and dry as a hen's egg. Her knitted cap covers hair
I've combed out with my own fingers. She comes to me

after rush hour, and we walk like in the movies, down alleys;
she recites poetry, she wears moonlight and neon like a crown,
and we eat whenever we please. Sometimes I find an empty dumpster,
not one near a restaurant but a business dumpster, one that held
shredded printouts, canceled checks and memos, fax paper, forms,
and we climb inside, concealed, sheltered, and make love. Once

when she was angry, she crawled out of the dumpster and beat
on the metal with an abandoned chair she found outside; thunder
whispers in comparison; it was the sound of absolute hell, utter
destruction; my head hurt for a week. I know I'm not the man

of her dreams. I'm King Lear on the heath, crazy, cold with
despair; I rave; my clothes are shabby. With my kingdom
divided, there are no more decisions to make, and my mind
gets weak. She is a scholar; I am afraid of books. I rave
and she listens to me, comforts me, tells me my daughter
will save me one day and I believe her.

HEOROT

for Thomas Thornburg

The epic form has natural extension,
grand thematics, intensified dimension
exceeding mundane space and time.

Only a poet could create this place.

> *Hold now and guard the best of houses:*
> *remember your fame, show your great courage,*
> *keep watch against the fierce foe.*

The streets shine in all weathers
in a town battered by trains.

The sidewalks are always empty.

The piano player wears a rhinoceros mask,
bends the beast-head low over the keys.

No one considers this odd.

> *Driven by need one must seek the place*
> *prepared for earth-dwellers, soul-bearers.*

Street people listen intently
to a student reading Corso.

Right on, man. That's the truth.

Time warps like the curve
in rising cigarette smoke.

The hangings on the walls shone with gold,
many a wondrous sight for each man.

Gilded helmet. Round shield.
Coonskin. Pheasant. Long bow.

Two headed axe. Three white skulls
with antlers still attached.

Deep red carnations.

Rattlesnake skin.
Jars of pickled sausage.
Moose rack touched with gold.

> *Then the woman went about to each one,*
> *young and old, offered the costly cup,*
>
> *until she brought the mead-bowl to Beowulf,*
> *the ring-adorned queen, mature of mind.*

The kerosene dragon glows in its lair.
Our hands touch at the edge of the table.

> *None remains with me*
> *to bear the sword,*
>
> *burnish the rich goblet,*
> *costly drinking-cup;*
>
> *the company has gone elsewhere.*

Time is the fiercest enemy
we have yet encountered.

Create a space for poetry.

> *You will not lack what you wish*
> *if you survive that deed of valor.*

A MASSING OF PLANETS

The screened porch faces north.
Petunias crushed by nightfall
trace sweet designs in humid air;
my breasts are heavy with sweat,
with breath held shallow by heat.

I am subject to memories that burn.

In the west, hidden by maples,
Venus moves close to Mars,
sparking a coordinate fire.

A faint breeze rises in the lilacs,
sheet lightning turns the trees black.
This is the weather of innocent climates,
where climax is gently withheld.

Jupiter swings near and settles;
Leo is crowded with alien bodies,
round and glowing, clustering,
demanding space. Burning space.

Night after night the planets gather,
the heat holds steady, and lightning
promises release. The rain does not come.

The screened porch faces north.
Petunias leave sweet scent suspended,
my breasts hang heavy with memory.
The twilight condenses against glass.

This conjunction ends with the solstice:
A red sun declines, three planets scatter,
wild hours of wind and rain commence.

SIDELING MOUNTAIN

Five bands of rock emerge like dolphins from beneath the sweet grass
of the interstate embankment, where trucks pass so quickly a riptide
of insects flows around their wheels. A rubble shoreline. A speckled
dolphin, a black dolphin, a dolphin grainy and trying to disappear.
Here the ocean swells to solid geometric waves. Arc of granite, arc of
shale, arc of sandstone, ark of the earth's mantle and all its
inhabitants, adrift, exposed to the light after breeding in the dark
shoals of time.

THE RAIN CROW

The rain crow builds her nest in the wind
knitting razors, blue glass bottles,
the clipped toenails of crippled children

her beak broken by steel, enamel,
barbed wire and stone, every hard
merciless beam, each riveted level

rising higher and harsher. She starts
to mourn before the eggs are laid,
keening, feasting on her own heart,

then shredding her flesh to stay
the hunger of the chicks, their vast
hurricane need. She calls the rain

to water her brood and the nest rusts,
the metals bleeding; the nest glistens,
the glass streaming. The soft brush

of a feather: electric tension
lines blistered black, chicks charred
dark, the lightning a lesson;

the wet wings blocking stars
absorbing light, bright eyes closed,
flying blind, bringing rain, the far

cold cry of the mother chilled low
and thin by the night, the children
with chipped nails, fledgling crows.

FLAMBEAUX

*... after sinking their drill several hundred feet, [they] struck gas,
but did not know what they had found; but from the roaring noise
produced by escaping gas, and the stench of the same, concluded
that they were perhaps encroaching on the territory of his satanic
majesty, and at once abandoned their project.*
         — *John S. Ellis*
          History of Delaware County (1898)

Three hundred million years ago, the midwest was at the equator.
A tropical sea flowed over Indiana, leaving behind the corpses
of innumerable small creatures, skeletons, calcium, lime.

In those days, continents drifted about like enormous icebergs,
so much of their substance beneath the surface,
hard rock and mountains buoyant and mobile
colliding to build great barren ranges
sinking to let the sea wash in
rebounding to lift the hardened sediment high,
the limestone and shale of the ocean floor
high and hot and dry as a desert

until the continents gathered in the polar regions
or the earth's rotational axis shifted, or volcanic activity
brightened the planet's albedo, and the ice formed

and reflected the sunlight and grew colder and deeper,
a terrible feedback loop layering ice upon ice
miles thick, ice as blue as fresh milk,
heavy and dense, steel strong and imperial
eating, grinding the earth down to powder
pervasive and unforgiving, relentless, ice.

Indiana was flattened by the ice; the Ohio River ran the outer limits
of several ice invasions; surge glaciers, lubricated by meltwater,
rushed down slopes at impossible speeds, leaving boulders
oddly scattered; alpine glaciers, reluctant and slow, carved out
valleys, leaving a whole lexicon of altered landscape,

bulges, moraines, drumlins, eskers, alluvium; and cap ice,
weary and brittle, moved south toward warmer weather,
breaking off into growlers, bergy bits, and brash ice,
bobbing like tiny continents finally out to sea.

In 1876, when George Carter came looking for coal,
he found instead the distilled remains
of marine life, a natural gas
released by decomposition, trapped in the rock,
the flammable soul of tropical Indiana
stored safely in skeletal stone.

Unrecognizable, unfamiliar, and smelling of sulfur,
the gas welled up and ignited.

In a world of grass and corn and open sky
the gas revealed an alien, subterranean,
explosive spirit.

When the gas boom began in earnest
ten years after Carter sealed the gate to hell,
jubilant boosters lit the gas and let it burn
day and night.

And the tiny sea creatures that waited
for the ice to retreat, their skeletons transformed
to shale and limestone, their soft tissue become gas,
the gentle unsophisticated plants, pressed into coal,
the carbon monoxide, the methanes and sulfides,
fermenting all those years beneath the ice,
tormented by tectonic forces, reduced to pooling
in pockets of porous rock, never seeing the sun,
never rocked by the sea's sweet waves, never
never again to be whole, skeleton and soul,
never again tropical, never saline, never warm

the small strange ancient creatures
responded to the drill as a call from a redeemer
rising up out of the earth, everything lost
everything exotic in Indiana burning
in flames that were visible
twenty miles away.

THE RESPIRATION OF THE PINES

Surrounded by a mist
that is their own breath
rising
the pines inhale blue sky
like divers surfacing
throats extended
droplets flying
as if a breeze
intervened.

The exhalation
of that great gasp
sweeps the weather
aside, clearing space,
an arm brushing
silverware
off the edge of a table
in an exaltation
of falling light.

Like monitor lizards
the pines stand alert
motionless inside the wind,
tasting the air with
needle tongues that drop,
silently
measuring purity,
volume, the density
of a breath.

TRINITY

He thought the atmosphere might catch fire.

Alamogordo. La Jornada del Muerto.
The MacDonald ranch. Ground zero.

The gadget suspended from a steel tower,
the blockhouse, broken clouds, countdown.
Sunrise. The goggles, the sand blowing,
instruments going wild, cameras, troops,
jeeps turning over, sunrise. Daylight.

Robert Oppenheimer grew thin at Los Alamos;
he faced a crisis of conscience. An implosion.

There was no demonstration and no blockade;
they dropped Little Boy on Hiroshima
Fat Man on Nagasaki. It was a scouring
and a statement. It was devastation.

He read John Donne's holy sonnets;
he read the Hindu sacred texts.

Trinity: father, son, spirit. Trinity:
Brahma the ineffable, Shiva, Vishnu.

Vishnu is the god of holocaust, of nuclear
winter, the stellar furnace, the sun god.

His avatar Krishna said to Arjuna:
go ahead and kill your kinfolk;

in the fullness of time all things die
and a warrior must be true to his nature.

Vishnu is the preserver of forms, the X-ray,
the shadows of victims burned into concrete,

endless uranium decay, scorched earth policy,
the plains of Carthage salted, Bikini blasted.

Arjuna hesitated in his chariot and Krishna insisted.

The Japanese starved at the end of the war.
Then came the light, the terrible heat, firestorm,
the rubble, melted glass, the walking dead, the pain,
the black rain, the sickness, mutation, sterility.

Everything was preserved on film.

Krishna invoked the endless cosmic serpent,
biting its tail in a frenzy of destruction;
he called Vishnu the purifying wind. He said:
the lucid, the splendid, the invulnerable,

all find their sources in fragments
of Vishnu's annihilating brilliance.

Arjuna praised Vishnu's devouring gaze
and learned to take the long view of time.

He gained a desire for apocalypse, for ashes,
saw the beauty in the fireball, heard music
in the roaring wind, felt caressed by shock waves
that flattened cities and splintered human bones.

He became a warrior true to his nature.

Picasso was 64 when the bombs fell.
He'd seen the Great War, Civil War,
the occupation of Paris. The camps.

Guernica. The Charnel House. The Dove.

When Oppenheimer was born in 1904
Picasso ended his Blue period, his
palette went Rose. He fell in love.
His colors kept pace with desire,
the physics of canvas, the optics
of invention, of carnal intention.

Les Demoiselles d'Avignon split vision
like an atomic pile; faces went planar,
odd facets exposed themselves; bodies
distorted the space around them, gravity
and time exploded, energy was released.

That was 1907; Oppenheimer was a toddler,
a good boy, delicate, very very smart.

There's a snapshot of Picasso sucking a fishbone
cleaning the skeleton with his tongue and his teeth;
later, he pressed the dry bone into clay and fired it:

the fish reappeared in a glaze of blue and green
swimming on the sides of a shallow bowl, preserved.

Shiva is the destroyer, the red one,
disintegration preceding creation.

Shiva is precious DNA, the double helix,
twins nested in the womb, the virus of life,
sperm and egg, yin and yang; looking both ways

he contends with black Kali, the ravenous woman,
he sows seed for Shakti, the mother, the witch

phallus and womb, fruit and vegetable, blooming,
ripe, rotten on the ground, his children bleed red.

Shiva consorts with the lowest, brings mud
and fungus glowing with decay to Shakti

sorcery, nudity, elemental energies,
the corrupt, the dissolute, the perverse,
the lotus growing in the swamp

flesh-eaters and scholars
the pregnant and the dying

he brings them all to Shakti,
and all are transformed.

Picasso might have dreamed him,
his four arms holding fire,
a drum, a horn, a trident,
dancing in a ring of flames,

his third eye shining
the three-eyed coconut
the fig and the banyan

the seeds of Rudra's eye,
the tears of the red god
who weeps for the world.

At the new moon festival
the devout cast dice

honor the ineffable
honor the paths of karma

honor Shiva and Shakti reconciled
the tenuous union of male and female

a contingent universe, bound by chaos,
waves and particles, radiant, spacious
mobile, contextual, sexual, graceful.

Shiva the auspicious one, Shiva the
lord of the dance, who stretches the map
of the shattered world, who brings order
to the formless, sends love to the lonely,
who scatters his seed to the four winds,

creator and destroyer, timely, fortunate,
snake-charming Shakti's coiled kundalini

howling out of the storm clouds, weeping
for the end of the world, dancing
in the circle of flames. Shiva.

Robert Oppenheimer died of cancer in 1967.

In August of that year, a 50-foot high sculpture
by Picasso was erected at the Civic Center in Chicago:

an enormous head: woman, horse, lion, or angel,
wings of steel flowing back, a latticework of struts,
space and shadow for bones, air for blood, open
to the rain and the ceaseless wind off the lake.

Picasso never named that sculpture.

Krishna and Arjuna are waiting
in Vishnu's golden chariot;

armageddon, apocalypse, revelation

Vishnu the golden, Shiva the red,
Brahma invisible and indifferent,

the Trinity test:
sunrise, sunrise,
daylight.

ABOUT THE AUTHOR

Patti White was a probation officer in Colorado before turning to academic life. She now teaches American literature at Ball State University and is the author of *Gatsby's Party: the System and the List in Contemporary Literature* (Purdue, 1992). Her poems have appeared in *Arts Indiana*, the *Hopewell Review*, *RedRiverReview* (e), *Forklift, Ohio*, *Literal Latte*, *The Ledge*, *The MacGuffin*, the *Mississippi Review*, *DIAGRAM* (e), *The Common Review*, *Nimrod*, and *THE HEARTLANDS TODAY*.

In 1994, she won the Hopewell Prize for Poetry for "Our Lady of Perpetual Help Business School" and, in 2000, first prize from Literal Latte (Food Verse Awards) for "The Love Zombies," and first prize in the MacGuffin National Poet Hunt for "The Elegant-Armed Anemone."

She has performed her work in a number of venues, including the Indianapolis Museum of Art, Taylor University, the Kellogg Writers Series, WBST public radio, the Carnegie Arts Center in Covington, Kentucky, and at the conferences of the Popular Culture Association, the Midwest Modern Language Association, and the Society for the Study of Science and Literature.

WHAT, PRAY TELL, IS AN ANHINGA?

Closely related to the cormorants, anhingas are
found in the Deep South — most commonly in
Florida. Our logo depicts an anhinga striking its
signature pose, a stance the bird must hold for long
stretches of time after each underwater fishing
expedition because, lacking oil glands to dry them
more quickly, its wings are too soggy to fly. The
sinuous anhinga is also known as the snakebird for
the way it swims with all but head and neck
submerged below the surface of the water.